G000111923

How to Wri

Copyright © Simon Haynes

Advice and tips from a full-time novelist

Bowman Press

www.spacejock.com.au

Version 1.02

Cover images copyright depositphotos.com

For info on new releases and updates:
spacejock.com.au/MLNF.html

A catalogue record for this
book is available from the
National Library of Australia

Contents

— 1 —

Introduction

I've been writing novels for over twenty years, but until recently I was never particularly speedy. My first novel took *forevah.* (Forevah is a technical term we authors use. I employ a lot of those.) Slowly, bit by bit, I learned about the craft, and each subsequent novel took me a little less time.

(I'll share my tips on writing novels quickly in a later chapter. That's not important right now.)

How fast you write a novel isn't the issue. What stops most people is finishing a novel. You get these terrific ideas, start writing, and then get bogged down after a few chapters. Maybe your characters are misbehaving, or your setting is kind of bland, or you've written yourself into a dead end and have no idea how to proceed.

Well, I'm here to help. Will my method work for everyone? That I cannot say. All I know is that several people begged me to write this guide, and it contains all my hard-won knowledge, along with many hints and tips.

I hope it's everything they asked for, and I hope it helps you too.

Regards

Simon Haynes
Perth, Western Australia

Before we begin

Do you want to try your hand at writing a novel, because it's something you've always wanted to do?

Or do you want a career as a novelist?

They're two very different things. With the former, you might have one idea for a novel, and you want to write it. You don't care if it takes years, you just want to write that one novel.

On the other hand, if you want to launch a career as a novelist, you don't care what the actual novel is about, or how many you have to write before (maybe) making a name for yourself. You're not wedded to a certain character, or determined to use a plot you came up with ten years ago but never got around to writing. You see novels as a product to make and sell.

Or maybe you have a foot in each camp: you have an idea for a novel, you're keen to write it, but if it works out you'd like to write more.

I can help with all of these scenarios.

2.1 The goal of this book

Quite simply, my goal is to get you to write a novel, from beginning to end. I'm not sure how long it will take you, because I don't yet know how many words you can write per hour, or how many hours a week you can devote to writing. We'll get to that later.

This may not be the first novel you've started – in fact, if you're anything like me, you've started dozens of the things. Just once, you'd like to type 'The End', and enjoy the feeling of accomplishment that comes with completing a very difficult undertaking.

Perhaps, like me, you're taking anything from two to five years to write each novel, and you want to work faster.

Or maybe, again like me, you're a compulsive re-writer, with twenty to thirty drafts being the norm. Instead of rewriting the same novel twenty times, you want to polish it once or twice, and then write another three or four novels with the time you've just saved.

Well, these are common scenarios, believe me. You'll notice I've suffered from all of them, and more besides.

I can pretty much guarantee that I've walked face-first into all the problems beginning, intermediate and even expert novelists struggle with. But I'm happy to report that I've overcome most of them, and I'm limping back from the wild frontier to report on my findings.

Does writing quickly mean I'm churning out words with no regard for quality? Actually, I write better when I'm working fast, because the entire novel is fresh and new in my mind. As for quality, I believe my novels are as good as I can make them, and that I'll only grow as a writer by writing more novels, not by writing the same novels at a much slower pace.

Finally . . . what are my credentials? Maybe I can write a novel or two, but are they any good? Only my readers can tell you that, and since they keep asking me to write more novels, I guess I'm doing something right.

2.2 The scope of this book

I like to be up front and honest with people, so here's a quick outline of what I think my book will help with, along with a list of topics that won't be covered.

The primary focus will be on writing your novel. That's what it says in the title and the description, and that's what I'm here to help with. I will also discuss plotting.

I like to give people more than they expect, so I'll also delve briefly into editing.

What won't be covered? I'm not the right person to teach grammar and punctuation, and I won't be talking about publishing either.

(You don't need to master grammar and punctuation to write a novel, but if they're a weakness I recommend hiring an editor to fix up your manuscript when it's finished. I've written a section on this in Part 4.)

2.3   Do you need yWriter?

Occasionally I will mention yWriter, my free software for novelists. You don't need yWriter to get the most out of this book, but it can be a great help organising your novel. Other writing software has similar features - just use whatever you're comfortable with.

yWriter is available for PC and mobile devices at www.spacejock.com/yWriter.html

/par

A Mac version is currently in progress, with an Alpha already available to download and test.

The mobile versions cost around five bucks, while the PC version is free to use.

2.4   Check the Appendix

Appendix I of this book contains a brief explanation of various terms I use from time to time. If you're new to novel writing you might like to check it out before continuing.

— 3 —

Plotting

In this part we'll take a very quick look at characters and setting.

After that, we'll go into the structure of a typical novel. Think of this as the underlying chassis or skeleton onto which we'll hang all those chapters and scenes we're going to write.

Then we're going to discuss your plot outline, whether you need one, and how to put one together. I'll also explain the hybrid method I use which combines elements of working with and without a plot outline.

3.1 Characters

Since novels are usually about people, it's vital to come up with living, breathing characters. Unfortunately, many authors think they have to do this *before* they write their novels, and they can get bogged down in detail before they've even started.

Yes, some people like to create their characters in detail before they start, with all the usual statistics like height, age, birthday, physical attributes, schooling, family tree . . . you name it.

Others start with a name and a rough age, and wing it. If you only invent details as you need them, you'll save a lot of time. Plus it's easy to go back after your first draft is finished, inserting a few minor details here and there.

I'm in the latter camp, because I like to introduce facts about the character only when necessary. For example, imagine I'm writing the first novel in a series, and I mention that one of my characters went to university in London. It's a nice little detail which tells us something about that character, even though it's just back story. However, I might have a plot in book four which requires that my character grew up in Australia instead, and because I threw in a casual piece of back story into the first novel I can't do it.

So, I like to keep my options open.

If you do write more novels featuring the same character, I recommend maintaining a biography for them, so you don't contradict yourself later. But if you're just starting a new novel, give yourself some freedom to improvise!

This is one area where beginning novelists can tie themselves in knots. Nobody has to read your first draft but you! You don't have to be consistent and accurate about your character's past at this stage, because it's trivial to go back when the manuscript is finished and fix things up.

Next, I'd like to talk about character motivations. Personally, I don't have 'good' and 'evil' characters in my novels, just people with opposite goals. The conflict this generates is more than enough to escalate things to a satisfactory climax and conclusion. I don't spend too much time developing bit players, unless they become more important during the writing. If someone's only going to appear in your book for one paragraph, treat them like a piece of furniture. Also, try and limit the total number of characters - sometimes you can combine two henchmen into one, for example - and if your book makes it into film, the casting people will thank you for saving them money. (Hey, it worked for

Sleuth.)

As a general rule your protagonist should be sympathetic - someone the reader can identify with. I realise that's difficult if you're writing about a serial killer, but in those cases the 'less is best' rule applies. As in, the less we see inside this monster's head, the more we fear them. If your killer becomes familiar and sympathetic, and the reader starts to identify with them, you've destroyed all the tension. That's why whodunits are called whodunits and not we-know-whodunnits.

3.2 Setting

The setting is the time and place where the actions in your novel occur. Each novel has one setting, but can have one or more locations. For example, your setting might be modern day England, and your locations might be the pub, a car park, the beach and so on.

For a time-travel science fiction novel the setting might be simply 'the Universe', but locations can still be defined as planet X 1000 years ago, planet Y in the future . . . you get the idea.

If your setting takes place across three countries, then your setting might be 'Europe' or 'South America'. It's not something you have to define, I just want to illustrate the difference between setting and locations.

As with characters, some writers like to know where every paving stone, every tree and every building is before they start writing, while others just start typing and add whatever features are needed as they get there.

Unless you absolutely must include real places in your novel, it's probably best to invent or rename them. First, if your characters are meeting in some cockroach-infested hotel you know of from real life, there's the possibility of come-back from the real-life owners, especially if they bought the place a year ago and have cleaned it up in the meantime.

And second, if you make places up, nobody can accuse you of getting things wrong. Science fiction authors have a big advantage here, for the time being at least.

3.3   Outlining vs pantsing

Outlining, or plotting, involves describing your novel in summarised form before you start writing it. A plot outline might be anything from half a dozen sentences to several thousand words.

Pantsing, or winging it, involves sitting down to write with only a vague idea where the novel is heading. You just start typing and see where it takes you.

Each has its own appeal, as the following examples demonstrate.

Imagine sitting in your car, knowing where you want to go, and only having the vaguest idea how to get there. You set off, and along the way you have the freedom to take side roads and short cuts ... which may turn out to be anything but. Maybe you spot a row of shops or a park you never knew existed, but eventually, with any luck, you'll arrive at your destination. How long will the trip take? No idea. How much fuel will you need? Not sure.

Contrast that to driving with a GPS, where a voice keeps interrupting your thoughts by insisting you take the second exit from a roundabout, or that you turn left in one hundred yards. Even if you're familiar with most of the journey, it will keep telling you where to go, and if you turn one street too early it will nag you until you correct your mistake. On the plus side, you'll have a very good idea of how long the trip will take before you set off, as well as an accurate idea of the overall distance.

If you want to enjoy the journey, don't care which route you take, and are in no rush to reach your destination, then pantsing a novel is a great choice.

If you're writing to a deadline and have a target word count in mind, outlining is the way to go.

3.4   Pros and cons of outlining

For me, the number one issue with outlining is that it strips a lot of the spontaneity out of the writing process. *Please note, I'm not suggesting outlining detracts from the finished novel!* What I mean is, when you write to a plot outline, you're rarely going to encounter anything unexpected or surprising. Sometimes a new character might appear out of nowhere, but generally you're following a well-worn path.

I don't want to labour the point, but writing to a plot outline is like reading the screenplay for a brand new blockbuster movie just before you watch it on the big screen. Every twist is telegraphed, and there's very little in the way of excitement.

So, if it dulls the fun, why would anyone want to use a plot outline?

First, and most importantly, it's much quicker to read, revise and rewrite a two page summary than a four hundred page novel. It's easier to spot flaws and it's easier to get an overview of the whole book.

Next, working to a plot outline means you can tackle

your novel quickly and efficiently. Every sentence you write should move the novel forwards.

Many authors get enjoyment from the technical skill of writing: choosing words with care, varying usage so they don't repeat themselves, using varying sentence lengths to avoid a dull, metronomic rhythm. With a plot outline you can focus on these things, instead of wondering why your major character just climbed a telegraph pole.

3.5   Pros and cons of pantsing

Writing a novel without a plot outline is akin to sailing a vast ocean without a compass. You set off and go wherever the wind blows you. Or maybe you're an explorer hacking through virgin forest with a machete, never knowing what you're going to find. It's exhilarating! It's exciting!

And it can also be exhausting, time consuming, and very inefficient.

I wrote my first four novels without an outline, and each one ended up 50,000 words over target, words which had taken hours and days to write, but now had to be chopped out and discarded.

That's 200,000 words, completely wasted. Or to put it another way, I could have written two or three additional novels. Not only did it waste time, I lost thousands in royalties as well!

So why would anyone write without a proper outline to guide them?

First-timers will probably work better without a plot outline. If you're still learning the craft and have never finished a complete manuscript, it won't hurt to inject a bit of excitement and discovery into the writing process. It can also lead to some truly unique works. As far as I know, Douglas Adams and Terry Pratchett weren't keen on outlining, instead letting their strange and varied characters take them by the hand and lead them wherever they wanted.

Pantsing can result in a first draft packed with a whole series of disconnected situations or events, linked by some overarching plot the author dreamt up along the way. This is why 'unplotted' novels often require extensive rewrites, and many drafts. All those ragged edges have to be filed down so the pieces fit neatly together.

Yes, I speak from experience. *One of my novels went through twenty-five drafts before I was happy with it.* That's 25 times I printed out, read and made changes to an 85,000 word novel. I could have written 12 more instead.

3.6 Writing a plot outline

I can't tell you how to come up with your story ideas and characters, because if I did we'd both end up writing similar novels. What I can tell you is that the best way to build a plot outline is to come up with a basic idea and flesh it out in more and more detail until you have a comprehensive plot. Run a web search for 'The Snowflake Method For Designing A Novel' and you'll find Randy Ingermanson's terrific article on the subject.

I created yWriter, my novel-writing software, back in 2002, and my software lends itself naturally to this style of plotting.

How? As mentioned in Appendix I, scenes are the building blocks of chapters, and of course chapters are the building blocks of your novel. If you tackle your novel one scene at a time, instead of worrying about the whole, you will find it much easier to handle, and that's where novel-writing software comes in. Every chapter, and every scene, has an area where you can write a brief, one line heading, and a box where you can type a description.

So, how do I create my outline? First, and most important, I decide how long my novel is going to be, and settle on a target word count. I know this seems backwards, but believe me, it makes creating your plot outline a whole lot easier.

My Hal Spacejock novels tend to be 85,000 words each, whereas my Harriet Walsh novels are shorter, at 55-65,000 words. Let's choose 75,000 as a mid point.

I know from experience that my chapters run to 2000-2500 words each, occasionally 3000. Therefore, our example 75,000 word novel will have roughly 30-40 chapters.

So, in my writing software I will create 36 blank chapters. I like to start with a number divisible by four, and I'll explain why in just a second. If you're using a regular word processor you can manually create 36 chapter headings - they don't have to have numbers, just write 'Chapter', duplicate it two or three times, then select them all and paste until you have the right number. Finally, select the lot and choose the 'heading' text style. If you view the document outline in your document it should just show the word 'Chapter' a bunch of times.

Now we're going to move to the ninth chapter in our document, and change it to 'Chapter 9 (Middle Part)'. Then we'll move to the 25th chapter, and rename it 'Chapter 25 (End Part)'

Now you should have eight chapters for the opening part of your novel, sixteen for the middle section, and eight for the end. This proportion is about right for a typical three-act novel.

If it all seems a bit paint-by-numbers, remember this: we're only putting together a plot outline. That is, a framework to pin your novel to. When you're actually writing the novel you'll find you will need to move things around, but for now we're starting with a blueprint so we don't try and fit the basement above the kitchen. A map, a blueprint, a rough outline . . . they'll all give you confidence to keep writing, to keep moving forwards.

Now that we have our outline document (which you can save as a template, to be reused for future novels), let's start with a really basic idea for a novel:

A woman discovers her husband has been kidnapped, and there's a note warning her not to call the police. She uses her initiative to trace his recent movements, discovers a couple of people who might have taken him - and why. With the help of a friend, she finds out where they're holding him, mounts a rescue operation, and gets him back.

I know it's very sketchy, but it's only an example. For now, imagine the three sentences in our outline above represent the 'beginning', 'middle' and 'end' of our novel.

You'll notice there's an awful lot missing, but this is just a very broad idea written down in two or three sentences. You're not supposed to take this and start writing chapter one. Well, not if you're writing to a plot outline at least. Pantsers can stop reading this section now, and head off to write their novels.

Okay, so the rest of you are still here. How do we turn those 2-3 sentences into a comprehensive plot outline?

First, don't get too hung up on the characters or the setting just yet. A lot of those details will come out as you're writing the novel, and the worst thing you can do is spend days agonising over the main character's hair color, or what kind of car they drive. Right now we're only worried about what happens in the novel.

Let's jump ahead for a second. What do you need from your plot outline? I'll tell you what you want, and that's a brief paragraph for every scene in your novel. But how do we expand our brief outline into a document full of detail? Like this:

A woman discovers her husband has been kidnapped.
Okay, well that's not much to go on for the first 8 chapters, or 20,000 words, of our novel. So let's expand on it by asking ourselves questions, and picturing the answers. As you do so, remember that novels are meant to have conflict. Always give your characters hard choices, with real consequences.

Where is she when she becomes aware of the fact?
Who else is there?
How does she learn about it?
What does she do?
Imagine a woman at work. Her husband has a job

where he's definitely going to be missed - let's say he's a high school teacher. It's mid-morning, and she takes a call from the school admin, trying to find out why her husband hasn't showed. The woman is immediately concerned, because she saw him leave for work.

Right now I can picture her sitting in an office in the city, maybe a high-rise, with the busy hum of co-workers all around. Maybe she's a bit of a go-getter, self-assured, and her husband is a bookish English teacher. When she takes the call, her first thought is 'auto accident', and because he drives the older car, she's worried he might have got hurt. She tells the school she'll call his cell phone and sort things out, but they tell her they already tried. (Right around now I'm considering an earlier scene, where the woman and her husband have breakfast together and chat about getting a new car. He's fond of the old one. She thinks it's unsafe.) The woman promises to ring around, apologises, the admin person hangs up.

Now we have a bit of drama, a bit of doubt, but nothing earth-shattering. The woman is stuck at work, but her husband is missing. It's out of character, but she calls a couple of his friends anyway, in case he's held up somewhere. Nothing.

Just to make things interesting, let's give her some drama at work to deal with. (You'll notice I haven't specified WHAT this woman does at work yet. That's where you'd draw on your experience, or that of people you know. Choose something you are familiar with, or can research easily.)

So, let's say a big client is coming in for a meeting, and our protagonist (the woman) has to be in that meeting. She knows this before the school rings her. If you bring this in afterwards, the reader will think it's just a bit too convenient. That's one of the skills involved in putting together an effective plot: building it brick by brick, foreshadowing, introducing small problems in passing, only for them to become major obstacles later. Always remember this: unlike the reader, you're not experiencing the novel in a linear fashion. You can jump back and forth adding detail wherever you like.

So, maybe this big fish of a client represents a huge portion of the company's turnover, is threatening to pull his or her business, and if they do, the firm will close down. Now we're piling the pressure on - missing husband, drama at work. Imagine how upset she'll be if her job ceases to exist, and her husband isn't in hospital, he's off at some strip club with his buddies?

We'll keep adding detail to this, until she finally has to leave work early and head home, to see if he's in bed sleeping off a bad headache or something. Maybe she finds the place has been trashed. She's about to call the cops when the phone rings. Someone tells the woman her husband has been taken, and she won't get him back unless she hands over the stuff. (What the stuff is . . . that's up to you. Cash, stolen goods, drugs, a compromising recording, whatever. It depends on the genre . . . it seems I'm writing some kind of thriller here, but your mileage will vary.)

I'm pretty sure the off-the-cuff ideas I've thrown together above could be expanded easily into eight chapters. By the way, don't fall into the trap of plotting out every car trip or subway journey, unless something important happens on the way. Travel is best omitted, which is one of the reasons we use scene breaks. After our character leaves the office, we add the ubiquitous *** and start the next scene with *As she pulled up in the driveway . . .* or *When she got home, she found the front door ajar . . .* You get the idea.

By now, the document we created earlier should have a paragraph or two under each of the first eight chapter headings. If the paragraph includes a change of location (skipping boring travel!) or a new character's viewpoint, I'll insert a *** marker to indicate there are two or more scenes in the chapter.

For example, we could have a scene at the school before the one with the woman at work, where the teacher (husband) is late for class and someone is sent to cover. A staffer is asked to call his wife, to see if he's sick. Then we cut to the wife taking the call. These two scenes have a viewpoint shift, and so they'd be split with the *** marker, as mentioned above.

I'm not going to go through the whole process with the middle and end of the novel because it's the same as creating the start. You'll notice I've come up with ideas for new scenes as I'm going along, even though they're not in logical order, and that's how I plot my novels. I'll go back and insert new scenes as they come to me, extending and expanding the document.

As you add these layers of detail, more and more ideas will come to you. Most writers think about their plot outline throughout every day (and night!), scribbling notes on scraps of paper, work documents, the backs of envelopes and so on. Although not every idea will make it into the plot, they're all valuable. Sometimes one duff idea will generate two really good ones.

One tip is to print out your plot outline from time to time, writing all the new ideas alongside, in between or right over the top of the existing entries, expanding and filling in the blanks. Once your printout is covered in scrawl it's time to fire up the computer and type them all back into the master copy of your plot. You'll come up with more ideas and notes during this process, which can all be typed into whichever application you're using to hold the plot outline.

Then, print it out and go for it all over again.

Over time your plot will grow into a complex and detailed document, until you know what happens, when it happens and who it's going to happen to. Now you're ready to write the book.

Remember, once you have an outline you don't have to stick to it! Your plot outline is just a guide, and if something unexpected comes up while you're writing a scene you can easily read the rest of the outline to see how the change would affect subsequent events. Every unplanned change creates ripples . . . sometimes they're confined to a single scene or chapter, and sometimes they'll have a big impact on everything to follow - and much of what came before. You have to decide whether it's better to stay on track or to take this new and interesting path. And there's your spontaneity.

3.7   A hybrid method

Okay, we've covered plotting and pantsing and there are writers who are firmly committed to each camp, but there is a third choice.

First, let's recap:

•It can be fun to write without a plot outline, because of the freedom. On the other hand it can take five or ten times as long to write a novel this way, and the rewrites are a big part of that.

•Writing plot outlines can be fun too, because it's like pantsing an entire novel in a few thousand words. On the other hand, writing a novel from a comprehensive plot outline can become dry and boring.

Wouldn't it be great if there was another way, where you still had fun but also got your book finished without all that wasted time and effort? That's where my hybrid method of writing a novel comes in, and if you get nothing else from my book, this next part should be worth the price alone. It's changed the way I approach my novels, and I've gone from writing one novel per year to writing and publishing four novels in the last four months.

They're not junk, either. The reviews have been overwhelmingly positive, and they're probably the best-received novels I've ever written.

So what's the trick?

Okay, let's take the short outline from the section on plotting your novel:

A woman discovers her husband has been kidnapped, and there's a note warning her not to call the police. She uses her initiative to trace his recent movements, discovers a couple of people who might have taken him - and why. With the help of a friend, she finds out where they're holding him, mounts a rescue operation, and gets him back.

Now, instead of expanding on this to create a comprehensive plot outline, we're going to try something crazy and radical. We're going to write the first two chapters of this novel!

Yes, I'm saying you should write around 4000 words of fiction without a detailed plot outline to guide you. By all means, flesh it out a bit first, but the idea is to just write and learn about your character, the setting, the challenges she's facing. See what happens! It might turn into a completely different novel at this stage, but so what? You haven't written an outline yet, so it doesn't matter!

Let's say you write four scenes: A husband and wife eating a hurried breakfast before heading off to work, with a minor dispute about trading in his old car. The woman arriving at work to learn about some major client coming in, disrupting the whole place. A scene at the school, where they're annoyed at some teacher for not showing up for work. They call his cell phone to leave yet another message, then decide to call his wife at work to check on him. Finally, the scene at work, where the woman takes the call about her husband.

In writing these scenes you'll be thinking and learning about the characters of the husband and wife, their respective workplaces and additional characters who might play a major role in the novel. (I'm already fitting up the big client or his associates as the person behind the husband's disappearance. In other words, it's to pressure her, not him.)

So, you now have two chapters and a brief plot outline. What next? I'll tell you what we're going to do now . . . we're going to stop writing and spend two or three days really nutting out the plot of our novel. This is where the previous section on plotting your novel comes in, because you want to end up with 4000-7000 words of detailed plot outline, with at least a paragraph per scene.

This plot document should be comprehensive, and you shouldn't start writing the rest of the novel until you're happy you've covered everything. Trust me, while writing the novel you'll get new ideas, and as long as they don't completely change everything, go with them if they're better. I strongly, strongly, advise against big changes, because that way lies madness. If you come up with an entirely new, better, plot . . . use it for another novel!

Now we have a start to our novel as well as a detailed plot outline. We're ready to write the rest of the novel, and I'll cover this in an upcoming chapter.

3.8 The structure of a typical novel

There are many different structures you can use with your novel, but this one works for me.

Beginning
- Create or choose your setting.
- Introduce the characters. (Not all at once. Bring them in slowly.)
- (Optional) Bring in the antagonist, and give them a goal.
- Give your characters a major goal, plus smaller ones. (This might just be 'stop the antagonist')
- Make your characters suffer. (Conflict!)

Middle
- Make sure your characters keep failing, albeit with some successes along the way.
- Lead up to a major event ... which is a disaster for our major character(s).

End
- They regroup, lick their wounds, approach the problem another way.

•Eventually, they overcome the major obstacle and achieve their goal.

If you boil down most books, plays and movies, they usually end up fitting into the structure I've outlined above. Why? Because it works! More importantly, it's what sells.

You may have to adapt this to suit your own novel, because this is only a framework to give you the idea of a three-act structure. Appendix I goes into more detail on the terminology I've used here.

— 4 —

Writing your novel

We have a plot outline! Or, if you're a pantser ... we don't! Either way, it's time to start writing your novel.

4.1   How many words in a novel?

Okay, it's *almost* time to write your novel.

I want to pause here, and mention novel lengths. A novel is understood to be roughly 40,000 words and up. Less than that and you're looking at a novella. Less than 7500 and you're talking about a short story.

So, does that mean you can write 40,001 words and call it a novel? Generally, no. If you publish a really short novel, readers might leave bad reviews complaining they were ripped off. (The only genre where this doesn't apply is erotica, where, ironically, longer is not necessarily better.)

So, once you know which genre you're writing in, I suggest you do a little research to find out what readers expect. Fantasy readers expect long books - 180,000 words is not uncommon. Science fiction is usually half that, maybe 75,000 and up. Every other genre has its typical novel length, and you'd be wise to come in at around the expected word count.

Back in the bookstore days, a thick book stood out on the shelves. You had this soap powder situation going on, where the bigger the spine the more sales, and a skinny little book had next to no chance.

With ebooks all of this has gone out the window, and the cover art, title and book description are now the biggest draw when it comes to getting attention. Some readers still check the page count on the product page, though, and if you have a high fantasy novel with a sum total of 120 pages it's going to hurt your sales.

So, do a little research, find out the expected page count for your genre, and use it as a guideline.

4.2 Keep moving forward

This is the key part to writing a novel.

When writing your first draft, aim to keep moving forward. Resist the temptation to rewrite existing chapters.

If you go back and make changes now, you'll not only interrupt the flow, you also run the risk of getting stuck on the Treadmill 'o' Wonder. This is where you run on the spot, muttering 'I wonder what it's like to finish a novel?' under your breath.

I estimate that only five or ten percent of those who start writing a novel actually finish the first draft.

This is what happens: You're writing chapter twelve of thirty-six, and you decide to change the setting. Maybe a different city, which is fairly trivial. So, instead of writing chapter thirteen, you go back to the beginning and start replacing 'London' with 'Paris'. This sounds harmless, but while you're re-reading your draft, you may come across a few places which aren't perhaps as well-written as you remembered them to be. Maybe they seem to drag a bit. (This is natural, by the way.

You not only wrote these parts, you've probably read them twice already. How can they seem anything but stale?)

Some people lose heart at this point, and give up. Others throw everything out and start over. Some will start rewriting and editing, introducing new and exciting ideas ... ideas which need wholesale changes to the twelve chapters already written ... *and* their plot outline, if they're using one.

Let's say a miracle occurs, and you arrive at chapter twelve having 'fixed' all the issues you spotted. You write chapters thirteen through twenty, and then ... decide to change the setting again. Or you want to add a new character. Or perhaps killing a certain character was all a big mistake, and now they're only wounded.

So, it's back to the beginning, and now you really are on that treadmill. I'm guessing the majority of unfinished novels are sitting on hard drives, unloved, because the writer kept fiddling with something he or she ought to have left well alone.

So, here's the fix. If you come up with a gee-whizz idea which requires changes to the portions you've already written, insert a note in the current scene, the one you're writing now, which says 'Change the setting to Paris'. Or 'Fred isn't dead, he's only stunned'. And then ... here's the good bit ... KEEP WRITING. And from that point on, treat your characters like they're in Paris, not London. Have Fred speaking and breathing.

I'll tell you why this is important: Five or ten chapters from now you'll have another bright idea ('The detective is female, not male' or perhaps . . . 'The novel is set in Sydney', or even . . . 'Maybe Fred is dead after all'). If so, insert another note and keep writing.

If you're using a word processor, just preface your comment with TK:. This letter combination is rare in English, if not completely unused, which makes it really easy to locate your notes and comments afterwards using a simple search for TK. In yWriter, you can include comments in your scenes by wrapping them in a certain style. This way they're not included in the word count, which is nice when you delete a bunch of comments and your word count *doesn't* start the day in negative figures!

So, you must focus on getting your first draft down. You need to get that manuscript finished, and you need to write The End. Those fix-ups we've been discussing in this section? They're editing and revision, not part of the writing process when we're trying to finish the first draft.

For some writers, leaving things 'unfixed' in their manuscript is like listening to the phone ringing on . . . and on . . . and on. Or perhaps it's a kettle boiling away in the kitchen, a nagging irritant that you just have to deal with before you can get on with the writing. I'm asking you to ignore those irritants and write on regardless.

4.3 How long will it take?

First, decide on a daily word count which you can manage easily. If you're not using a plot outline, just estimate the finished length of the novel and divide it by an arbitrary number of days. We'll fine tune this later.

I use yWriter to estimate the number of words I need to write per day, because I can enter the total word count of the novel (say, 75,000 words), and the date I want to finish on. (Say, 30 days from today.) yWriter will then tell me I need to write 2500 words per day. If I don't write anything on day one, tomorrow yWriter will tell me I have to write 2586 words per day. If the daily word count is too high, just push back the ending date by a week or so. If I write more than the required count, the figure will be adjusted downwards automatically.

It's not unusual to reach the last couple of chapters of my novel, only to have yWriter tell me I need to write 200 words per day for the next week to finish off. This is good . . . it means I'm well ahead of schedule, and for my next novel I will make the deadline a little shorter.

On the other hand, if yWriter is telling me I need to write 9664 words per day, I've wildly underestimated my writing speed. I will need to allow myself more time in future.

Finally, if yWriter informs me I need to write 75,000 words in a single day to finish the manuscript, I know I'm a slacker who never got started in the first place.

If you're just starting out I'd aim for 500 to 1000 words per day. I can occasionally type 4000 words of fiction in an hour, but I've been doing this for over twenty years. If you can type 500 words of fiction per hour, then you will finish your 75,000 word first draft in 150 days, or just under 5 months. I'm being really conservative with numbers here, because even if you type with the old two finger hunt-and-peck method, and achieve 10 words per minute, one hour should net you 500 words no problem. On the other hand, most of us type a fair bit thanks to emails, reports for work, school, you name it, and I believe 500 words in half an hour should be achievable for most.

It doesn't really matter. If you could give up one hour per day, maybe in two 20-30 minute sessions, wouldn't you do it, if it meant you could write and publish two novels per year?

4.4 Writing with no plot outline

Excellent! Today is going to be a mystery tour, because you have no idea where your novel is going.   If you followed my suggestion, you wrote down a few sentences describing the plot of your novel, but you skipped all that boring, mood-killing effort involved in writing a detailed outline.

So, how do we start? What are we going to put in chapter one?

I'll tell you how we're going to start: we're going to write down two or three sentences detailing what this scene is going to be about. I'm not kidding, we really are going to put down a mini plot outline, but *it's only for this scene.*

If you think I've just pulled a trick on you, relax. All I'm really asking you to do is think the scene through before you write it. What's going to happen? How's it going to end? We need that much at least, otherwise we're just pouring word soup on the page.

It shouldn't take long, so open up the word processor

and type something like this. (I'm going to write this off the cuff, here and now.)

Husband and wife having breakfast. She's late for work, maybe wearing business clothes, he's much more casual. She's flipping through the morning paper while she tries to gulp hot coffee, and sees a full page ad for a new car. Shows him, he pulls a face. He's a teacher, he can't show up in something like that.

She grabs a briefcase and gets in her sleek new car, some euro model, which is parked next to an old pickup or similar. Even as she drives off, her workplace calls with news of an urgent meeting later that morning.

Okay, that's my outline. I could turn that into a chapter no problem, throwing in more detail and of course, dialogue. My point is, even if you're not into outlines, writing down what you're going to say, before you actually say it, is a great way to prepare yourself for the task ahead.

Now, because you're pantsing, you don't really know where this woman works, whether the husband has a day off, what this business meeting is about ... nothing! The next chapter or scene is still a complete mystery.

Okay, so you finish writing this scene and you're all keen to do more. Maybe you've finished watching everything on youtube, or you want to have your novel finished in weeks, not months. Move to the next chapter and ... write an outline for the next scene.

Of course, you don't actually have to type the outline each time. You could just keep it in mind while you write the scene. But the mini outline is great if you're writing the scene over one or more days. Re-reading that mini outline is a lot quicker than reading every word of your novel.

So is that really my suggestion? Writing with no plot outline involves ... writing a plot outline first? Well, sorta kinda. The only difference is that you're plotting the scene you're about to write, not the whole novel. You have total freedom, unlike that other author with their strait-jacket of a plot outline which they can't deviate from.

4.5   Writing from a plot outline

Your comprehensive plot outline is the rails.   The stations are your chapters. You are the train. As long as you keep going, you will pass each station and reach your destination. You can't miss, not unless you fiddle with the points and divert your train into the nearest gulch.

Don't fiddle with the points.

If you stick to your plot outline, your journey will be smooth and uneventful.   On the way you'll pass legions of pantsers hacking away at jungle thickets, wading waist-deep through swamps full of alligators, or pedalling their bikes through snow storms. Make the most of it, because they'll thin out after the first couple of stations, and further down the line you probably won't see them any more.

When writing from a plot outline you can avail yourself of a rare luxury: you don't have to write your chapters and scenes in order.

This trick requires a little bit of experience, because you need to be able to read your plot outline, and estimate roughly how many words each chapter or scene is going to need. For example, in the previous section I mentioned a breakfast conversation between husband and wife. I know from experience that I'd be looking at 1500-2000 words to adequately write that scene. There is no way I'd rush through it in 500 words, and I wouldn't stretch it to 3000, either, not unless I was describing every stitch in their clothing and quoting chunks of the daily paper the protagonist was reading.

As I said, this estimate comes from experience. It also depends how the plot outline was written. Does it contain a lot of fluff? Descriptive detail, instead of events? If so, the final word count will be shorter than it would be for a plot outline which really packs in the events. Take these two sentences:

Protagonist shoots a mugger in self defence, and is arrested and taken to the station.

or

Protagonist confronted by a mugger.

The first is easily 1500-2000 words, what with the mugging, the police showing up, explanations, the arrest, processing the protagonist, etc.

The second could be a single sentence. "Hand over your phone and your wallet!" At most, I can picture a 500 word scene where the protagonist is being shadowed - or is surprised - by a mugger. Presumably the next scene involves the shooting, the cops and so on. (If it's in this scene, it should have been in the outline!)

So, what was that luxury I mentioned? Well, if your document has the outline neatly split up under all the chapter headings, you don't have to write your novel in order. If you have half an hour to spare, you can sit down and write a 500 word scene, finishing it off before shutting down the computer. If you have more time, write one of the longer scenes. Sometimes it's best to start your writing day by tackling a short scene first. I did that today, whilst writing this book.

It's even easier if you have multiple viewpoint characters in your novel. You can write several scenes from one viewpoint, then interleave them with the other viewpoint characters later. When I switch between characters I like to stick with roughly the same timeline. If events are taking place on a Sunday, all my viewpoint characters will be experiencing events on Sunday. When the plot ticks over to Monday, I don't stick in some scene where a character is still living out Saturday's events. They don't have to be sequential, and it can be effective to write overlap scenes, where you see the same events from two different characters' points of view, but I don't like to jump around all over the calendar because the reader will get confused.

Is that really it? The answer to how to write a novel is to break it into chapters and scenes, work out what's going to happen in each one, then type them out?

Well yes, boiled down to the minimum, that's it, but

that's like saying the only thing you need to play a song on a guitar is to hit the right notes at the right time. So, we're going to talk about pacing next.

4.6 Pacing

No, I don't mean walking up and down while you wait impatiently for the royalty cheque. (Or check . . . I don't care how it's written as long as my name is on the top line.)

Pacing is an important consideration. Consider a big-budget action movie. Do they light the fuse in the opening shot, and run at a million miles an hour until the credits? No, it would be exhausting. Plus going at a million miles an hour all the time is like rampant over-use of CGI . . . you get used to it pretty quickly, and then you start to ask yourself if there's anything of substance beneath the cool graphics and flashing lights. (Spoiler warning: usually the answer is an emphatic "no".)

You don't want to write a novel where every sentence is an explosion, a gun shot, a narrow escape or a man in tights punching a building or a moon or something. Constant action is hollow and unrewarding.

Instead, we write a scene with a Big Moment, and then we follow it up with a rest. The big moment can be a first kiss, an explosion, a surprise, a plot twist, a death, good or bad news ... anything which can be considered a major plot point.

Imagine a straight line drawn across the screen. Now we're going to add little hills to that line, representing Big Moments in our novel. They shouldn't be too close together, and they shouldn't be miles apart either. You don't want a cluster of them, because that just means the rest of the plot might be a little flat.

Actually, yWriter can help with this, because not only can you assign a rating from 1-10 in any of four different categories, per scene, but you can also view a chart of the values across your entire novel. I use it to rate the humo(u)r in my comedy novels, and if I see a couple of scenes in a row with low scores, you can bet I'll go in there and ramp them up.

You can also use these scores and charts to rank the danger level to your main character, or the Big Moments mentioned above.

But here's the thing: You want a Big Moment near the beginning (preferably something interesting in the first scene, to hook the reader), and after that you want these moments to get more intense as the novel progresses. It's like a firework display: they always save the biggest, most elaborate sequence until the end. Before that, we get pauses in between slightly lesser displays of noise and colour.

The pacing in your novel should be similar: A series of high points, which steadily get bigger until the last chapter or two, when they go off the scale. After that, the novel winds down to the end.

If you put all the fancy explosions (or Big Moments) at the start, the rest of the novel will seem drab and dull. If you save them all until the very end, most readers won't persist that far. Don't let all this talk of explosions get in the way: in a romance novel, the same effect occurs with all those will-he, won't-he moments, those misunderstandings where both sides retreat from a possible relationship, hurt or angry, or the appearance of a new rival for someone's affections.

Whatever your chosen genre, you will have dramatic events of some kind. I'm advising you to spread them out, and to build up to the biggest events. This, rather than going off with a bang and then following it up with thirty-five chapters of whimper.

4.7   My one-day-workout

Okay, somehow you've cleared an entire day in your schedule, and you don't want to waste it. You want to get a ton of work done on your novel, but if you're anything like me you'll procrastinate most of the day. First thing in the morning you'll review everything you've already written, to 'get in the mood'. At 1pm you'll decide to make lunch. After that it's 'research' (usually on Youtube or Netflix), and later in the day you decide to clean the house and cook a three course dinner.

Around 10pm you review your word count for the day ... not much, if anything ... and force yourself to write for an hour or two, ending up with a thousand words to show for your efforts.

You may be different. You might be fantastically organised, and have no trouble writing five or six thousand words if given a day's peace. If so, congrats, because you're a rarity.

For the rest of us, we have to structure the day a little. That's where my one-day workout comes in. I don't recommend using this method every day, it's just for those occasions where you have time to write and want to get on with it.

Here's what you do: Grab a sheet of lined paper and write times down the left-hand side, from 8:00am through to midnight in hourly increments. (You can use your own start and end times.)

In the next column, alongside each hour, write 500, 1000, 1500, 2000 . . . adding 500 words per hour.

At this stage I should point out that you can download a slightly more complex PDF version of this document from my website:

spacejock.com.au/files/NanoHourly.pdf

Note: If you can't write 500 words of fiction per hour, change the multiplier. Use 200, 400, 600 and so on. If you *do* change this figure, just use your own value everywhere I mention 500 words in the rest of this section.

Anyway, here's how it works: Starting with the first hour, sit down and write 500 words of your novel. It might take a while to get going, but as soon as you have roughly the required amount, set aside the word processor and do something else for the rest of the hour. But first, set an alarm for the top of the next hour (9am, in my example). Watch youtube, read the news, cook breakfast, make a coffee . . . just be sure you can hear that alarm.

When the alarm goes off at the start of the next hour, sit down and write the next 500 words. Stop when you've completed them and use the rest of the hour to do whatever you want.

I guarantee the first two lots of 500 will be the hardest, because it's tough to get writing at the start of the day. After that, you'll discover the 500 words goes pretty quickly each hour, although after six or eight of them it will start to take more and more time, until late in the day you might be using almost the entire hour to knock out the 500 words. You'll get a few minutes to fetch a drink, and then the alarm will go off again.

It can be a certain form of torture, this, which is why it's a one-day catchup, and not a daily routine.

However, if everything goes well, by the end of your working day (say, 15 hours?) you will have 7500 words of fiction. Even if you quit after ten hours, that's still 5000 words, and you can spend the evening cleaning the house. Bonus!

4.8 So you've got writer's block.

I'm going to cover writer's block under the chapter on fears, but here are two quick suggestions if you find you simply can't write a word:

1. Do a bit of outlining for the scene, until it leads into actually writing it.
2. Lie down, close your eyes, play the scene through in your head.

And here are a few more I use when I'm really particularly lazy:

3. They're going to jail me in thirty minutes if I haven't written 200 words.
4. No more coffee until I've written a scene.
5. Buy something nice. Display it above the computer. Get it when I finish the next chapter.

Rewriting and Editing

In this chapter I'm going to talk about revising your novel. That is, working through one or more drafts until the manuscript is done.

After that I'll discuss the types of editing, editing your own work, getting friends and fellow authors to 'beta' read your novel, and paying editors to fix flaws.

5.1 Revising your novel

Okay, the first draft is done. Have a coffee and/or snack of your choice, pat yourself on the back, and get ready for the best part. Revisions!

This is where you mould your lump of clay into a vaguely novel-shaped sculpture, but remember it's still a draft so don't expect the Venus de Milo. (Actually, perhaps you should, given her missing arms.)

It's a huge accomplishment, getting that first draft through to completion, and it's tempting to rewind to the first page and embark on the rewrites straight away. Resist the temptation! It's best to leave the manuscript for a few days. Do something else. If you're really keen you can start plotting another novel, although I wouldn't start writing it until your first is completely finished.

During those rest days you'll probably think about your plot, and you might even get a few lightning bolts of inspiration. Maybe there's a plot twist you can introduce, or maybe a character who's been helping your protagonist can actually be working against her.

That's fine, just write these ideas down. Tomorrow you might get an even better one.

Once you've given the first draft a few days rest, it's time to start on the revisions. The first pass through the manuscript is probably going to involve the most work, because you're going to be dealing with all those notes and comments you left around like so many traps. Now that you've finished the draft, some of the changes might not be as useful (or as relevant) as they were when you wrote them, in which case you can remove the comment and move on.

Eventually you'll reach a major one, such as changing the gender of a character or moving the novel to a different setting. There's nothing for it, you're going to have to re-read the novel up to that point, marking every required change.

How do I do this? I always, always print a hard copy of my draft. I sit down, away from the computer, red pen in hand, and I insert changes, scrawling between the sentences, in the paragraph breaks and all over the back of the pages. (If there's no room for a comment I put a letter inside a circle, write PTO, then put the same letter inside a circle on the back of the manuscript page along with the comments or corrections.)

So that I'm not carrying two stacks of paper everywhere I go, I fold over the corner of the first page and move it to the back of the manuscript. Then, as I write on each page, I move them to the back also, keeping them in order. Once that first page with the folded corner shows up, I know I've gone right the way through the manuscript.

Now, sometimes a scene needs so many changes it's going to be quicker to rewrite it, especially if it's a short scene of 500-800 words. If that's the case, I'll write a sentence or two of outline on the manuscript and put a big diagonal line through the scene.

While reading through your draft, take a note if your attention begins to wander. If you're reading a scene and thinking about completing your tax return, that scene probably needs some work. Maybe trim the sentences down, making them shorter and snappier. Maybe condense a piece of dialogue between two characters. It's amazing how much better something flows when you cut out excess words.

By the end of the process you'll have a manuscript covered in scrawl. Now for the fun part - it's back to the computer so you can apply all the changes!

For my first four novels, I would enter my corrections, rewrite any scenes which needed it, and then print the whole draft again. I'd get hold of the red pen and go through the whole process over and over, until I could read a draft without making any changes. (For the final draft, I'd leave the pen on the desk. I would only allow myself to pick it up for typos and errors, not minor changes to sentences.)

Wasn't that a huge waste of paper? Not really - I gave away signed, corrected pages from these manuscripts to people who attended my book launches!

Nowadays I just print the one draft, and then read through the manuscript on the computer for subsequent drafts. I don't do book launches any more, either!

5.2   The three types of editing

There are three types of editing, and they're very different. Some writers have made the mistake of paying for the 'editing' of their novel, only to receive a detailed report on their plot and major characters, when they were expecting to have their manuscript proofed and corrected and ready for publication.

So, what are the three types of editing?

1. Structural editing

2. Copyediting

3. Line editing and proofing

5.3 Structural editing

Structural editing is the most complex and expensive type of editing there is. Most indie authors don't hire editors for this, because they'd never make their money back in sales.

Four of my novels underwent structural editing when they were picked up by a trade publisher, and it's a comprehensive and exhaustive process.

Basically, a structural edit involves paying a professional to study your novel and find the flaws in the plot and the characters. It's a bit like a movie review, only in far more depth. As with a movie review, you may agree or disagree with the report.

A good editor will highlight the flaws, and it's up to you to fix them. One of the things my editor used to pull me up on was making my characters jump through hoops for various plot reasons, when there was an easier option. I would have to remove the easy choice first, forcing them to take the harder choice that I wanted them to take in the first place.

As an example, maybe I want my characters to do

some difficult maintenance on their spaceship, in a vacuum. I need this scene so that one of them can drift off into space, leading to a tense rescue. My editor would ask ... isn't it easier for them to fly to a nearby space station and fix the ship in safety? So, I'd add a little foreshadowing to make sure the engines were broken, or they'd run out of fuel or money. To paraphrase Sir Arthur Conan Doyle: when you eliminate the easy choice, whatever remains, however improbable, is the only one available to your protagonist!

As mentioned earlier, most authors don't pay for this kind of editing because it's too expensive. It's the sort of thing you just have to work through on your own.

Structural editing can improve your novel no end, but it could end up being the difference between a bunch of three star reviews, and four and five stars. Personally I'd rather write more novels and learn to improve my craft.

5.4 Copyediting

You know how your character started the novel with green eyes, but somewhere along the way they became blue? That's part of a copyeditor's job, along with grammar checking and ensuring you're consistent throughout the novel.

Copyediting, like structural editing, won't make or break your novel. It's a step that trade published novels go through, but most self-published authors do it themselves.

5.5   Line editing and proofing

Checking your spelling, fixing errors in punctuation ... line editing and proofing cover these and more.

If a self-published author seeks outside help, proofing is usually what they're after. However, as I've said earlier, you can try using your word processor's built-in tools to fix many of these errors.

One tip for catching typos and missing words: try changing the margins on your document, making the text on the page narrower. The eyes can miss errors near the sides of the page, so changing the margins will re-flow the document, giving you more of a chance to catch them.

Another trick is to listen to your novel aloud. Either read it to yourself, or use text-to-speech software like my own yRead3. It's amazing how easy it is to catch a misplaced word when you hear the sentence spoken.

5.6 Using Beta readers

A beta reader is a kindly soul who will read your finished, ready-to-publish novel, wait until the day before your launch, and then send you an exhaustive email tell you everything that's wrong with it.

Okay, I'm kidding! I have several beta readers and I cherish every one of them. A couple of them give me general feedback, while another is a demon with plot holes and typos.

So, a beta reader could be a friend, or family, who will read your novel and let you know what they think. Obviously this can lead to some pretty stony family gatherings afterwards, so I recommend using . . . I mean, asking . . . complete strangers to beta read for you.

How do you find them?

If you've published novels before, it's likely someone has emailed you about them. If you have a fan like this, why not ask them if they'd like a free copy of your new novel? Let them know you're after feedback. Some people are thrilled to be asked.

Alternatively, if you have a facebook page or a twitter account, maybe post a public request for a beta reader. Otherwise, try a local writing group.

A beta reader isn't usually a professional editor. It helps if they're a keen reader, and it helps even more if they enjoy the genre you're writing in. There's not much point asking someone to beta read your slasher horror novel if they only like romance or high fantasy. I mean, they can help with typos, but if they've never read horror before their feedback may not be that useful.

Now, once someone says yes, there are a couple of things you need to get clear. First, explain what you want from them. Proofing? General feedback? A list of plot holes or mistakes?

Next, let them know your release date, so they have an idea of when you need to hear back from them. And finally, let them know you want to hear all their thoughts, no punches pulled.

This is very important. It's a thousand times better to get some negative feedback from one or two beta readers before your book is released, than from dozens of paying customers after it's released.

Yes, it's nerve-wracking waiting for feedback, and if they send you a big list of problems with your novel it can be very confronting. Resist the temptation to write back and argue every point. If you do that, you'll lose the beta reader. Just take what you can use from the feedback and ignore anything you don't agree with.

Sometimes you won't hear back from them at all,

which isn't surprising. People have their own lives to lead, and reading an entire novel represents a decent chunk of time.

Oh, and always say thanks, and be sure to mention them in your acknowledgements.

— 6 —

Facing our fears

6.1 I'm no good at spelling and grammar

Neither of these will stop you writing a novel. Like I've said several times, nobody has to read your early draft.

If your spelling is a bit dodgy, you have a couple of choices. First, and most obvious, you can use the spell checker in your word processor to catch most errors. Second, you can hire (or beg) someone to proof your work. I've already spoken about clarifying your goals when you ask someone for help, so there's no need to cover that again.

Nobody expects published works to be 100% error-free. It's just not possible, and something will always slip through. However, frequent errors can distract readers so much they won't finish the book in question. Often, they'll leave a negative review, warning others. The worst thing about those is that even if you fix all the errors and upload a new version, the original review remains, like a permanent stain on your work.

Some authors resort to deleting their original novel and re-publishing it, sometimes with a different title and cover art. The problem with this approach is if one of your original readers accidentally buys the same book again . . . and leaves an even more negative review.

You can also check for grammar errors in your word processor, with varying degrees of success. It can be useful to catch some mistakes, but usually it won't detect clunky writing or incorrectly formatted dialogue. Again, having someone read your work can be a help, but if you're not paying a professional there's no guarantee the fixes will be any better than the original.

6.2 Fear of the empty page

We all experience this one. It's time to start writing for the day, and there in front of us is a nice, big, empty page.

First tip: when you stop writing for the day, end in the middle of a sentence rather than at the end of a scene. At least that will give you a thread to pick up the following day.

Here's another tip: When you're starting on a fresh page you probably know *what* you need to write, especially if you've followed my advice and put together a rough outline. So, instead of launching into the scene, why not expand a little on the outline first? Just write a few lines telling yourself how the scene's going to begin. Type them right there in the scene, don't go off and write them somewhere else. You can always delete these sentences at the end of your writing session.

When I write, I picture myself right there in the scene with the characters, but it takes a little time for me to fade out my real life surroundings and fade into the story. That process is helped a lot by writing a few lines of preamble, until what I see and hear is transferred to my fingers, and from there to the screen via the keyboard. Once I'm in full flight I just type and type, living through the scene I'm writing, and the words pretty much flow by themselves until I hit the end of the scene.

Think of it as a warmup exercise. Getting into the zone like that is not always easy, which is why writing a few sentences of outline can help to break down the barriers between the brain and the screen.

Plus, as an added bonus, those first few sentences occasionally throw up a neat idea which is better than the one in your plot outline.

6.3 Fear we'll run out of ideas

Another common fear is that we don't have enough material for a full length novel. Maybe the plot seems a bit thin, or there aren't enough characters, or we have no idea how to fill the spaces between major plot events. Having our characters sit around and discuss what to do next isn't the answer.

There's a simple answer to this, and it's the reason we put together a plot outline.

I aim for 2000-3000 words per chapter. Usually that's two scenes, sometimes a long scene ending on a minor cliffhanger, followed by a shorter reaction scene which ends on the chapter hook. Sometimes it's just one long scene, maybe a pivotal point in the novel. Either way, I know that I work best to that length.

So, if I want to write a 75,000 word novel, I know I'll need roughly 32-36 chapters. Let's say 36 to keep the math nice and simple.

Breaking this down further, a typical novel is usually split into 1/4 of the word count for the beginning, 1/2 for the middle, and the remaining 1/4 for the end. Using my example above, I know that I'll need 9 chapters for the beginning, 18 for the middle, and 9 for the end.

In reality the chapter count will vary in order to fit the story, rather than the other way round. ("I'll have to cut this pivotal scene that wraps up my novel, because I've already written nine chapters in this section." Yeah, right.)

So our job is to make the first nine chapters, or roughly 20,000 words in my example, end on a major hook which leads into the rest of the novel. If you think of this section as episode one of a new TV series, you won't be far off the mark. Introduce the characters, give them one or more problems or conflicts to handle, show them handling those problems (and most likely failing), and then bring in the major whammy which is going to change their lives.

Again, there are hundreds of variations on this, and I'm not here to tell you how to structure your novel. I just want you to think of that opening section as a separate part of your novel, because if there's one thing I've learned over the years, it's much easier to break a big task into smaller ones, and tick them off bit by bit.

By the time you've written the opening section you'll know roughly how many words it takes you to handle events in the plot. For example, if you discover that one page of plot outline equates to ten thousand words of fiction, then your plot outline should be eight pages for an eighty thousand word novel.

This is a simplistic way of looking at it, because your plot outline may contain a sentence like "and then they save the world", but I think we both know what I'm getting at. If you outline at a consistent level of detail throughout, then your plot outline should equate to finished word count. Even if it's only within 20% either way, surely it's better to have this rough estimate than none at all?

So, when outlining, avoid getting into truly nitty-gritty detail, and avoid plonking down massive great events in one or two lines.

The middle and ending sections can be dealt with the same way as the opening, taking each as a separate part of the whole and working on them individually. If you do it this way, you'll quickly learn whether your plot outline is detailed enough, with enough material to carry the novel, or whether it's too detailed, with more subplots and characters than you can cram into the available space.

Either way, over time you will learn to estimate the finished word count of your novels using the length of your outline, and that's invaluable because it means you'll already know if you have enough material before you begin.

6.4 Fear that we're not real writers

This is irrelevant. Nobody else is going to read our first draft or our plot outlines unless you ask them to.

We're just writing for ourselves at this stage.

You can't build a wooden table unless you have enough lumber. You can't edit, polish and sell a novel until you've written the first draft. So think of your first draft as a bunch of rough lumber, and don't get hung up on the knots and splinters. It'll buff out!

6.5   Fear of being wrong

How can anything be 'wrong'? You're writing fiction!

That said, if you use real places in your novel, and you're not familiar with them, you'll need to do some research. For example, having your characters experiencing a particularly icy winter in Sydney, Australia, during the Christmas holidays, will have Australians rolling around on the floor laughing their assets off. Right after they chuck your book in the nearest dunny, and just before they leave a string of 1 star reviews.

On the other hand, when it comes to characters there is no right and wrong. You invented them! If someone doesn't like the way your characters react in a given situation, let that person go and write their own novel with their own characters.

6.6   Fear of writer's block

Yep, some people will avoid starting on their novel *in case* they get writer's block. They're so afraid of failure they never begin.

First off, don't tell all your friends and colleagues you're writing a novel. That'll cut the pressure by about 3000% because now it's your own private project. (Telling your partner is probably a good idea, or they'll wonder who you're typing 2000 words to every night.)

Second, writer's block is a bit of a catch-all excuse. If I get stuck in the middle of a novel, it's not because I'm fed up with writing, it's because I don't know how to proceed. One trick is to go forward a chapter, and write on from there. Leave the troublesome section until the revision stage.

First, create blank chapter headings for the next few chapters.

Now add 2 or 3 blank scenes to each. Don't worry about how long these are going to be, or whether you need one or four of them per chapter. You're just showing your brain the small steps involved.

Starting at the blocked chapter, jot down one-line descriptions for the blank scenes. You're just filling empty spaces right now, so it doesn't have to be amazingly exciting.

As you progress you might find yourself moving away from your plot. If it's more interesting - good. (As I said, writer's block is usually the result of trapping your characters in a dead end.)

Suddenly you will write down a scene description which makes fanfares sound, bells ring, etc. You know how this one goes! Don't write it immediately, just write more detailed notes for it. Over the next day or two it will stick in your mind, and you'll be able to refine it. Hold yourself back and don't write it yet. If you like you can stop outlining other scenes now. Instead, go away and play this vivid scene through your mind. If you're itching to write it down... well, there goes the writer's block! Never forget this: You're writing a novel, not reading one. What happens next is completely in your hands, but it's this freedom which can make you freeze like a rabbit in the headlights. Do you leap to the left or the right?

When you sit down to write this stand-out scene it may not be as grand as it was in your imagination. Don't worry, that grandness will come after multiple revisions. You will probably rewrite the whole thing several times before your book is complete - and this section is about un-blocking the creative juices, not writing a first draft which just happens to be the best novel the world has ever seen.

After you've written that stand out scene (SOS) you can go back to modify the scene descriptions leading up to it, perhaps adding references to events in the SOS. As you're rewriting these descriptions you will come across one which rings bells, sounds fanfares, etc. That's the next one you should focus on.

The moral of the story is ... write scenes which are busting to get onto the page, and skip the ones which seem like a chore. If you're bored out of your skull writing them, how's your reader going to feel?

Another tip: there's no need for long, boring transition scenes. For example, you have a character in London who needs to travel to Sydney. Unless something happens on the plane, you can end the London scene by hailing a cab for the airport. Then you can start the next with a quick mention of Sydney, just to orient the reader. Use the same trick on any other boring parts and your novel will fly along ... and so will you.

6.7 Finding time to write

250 words per day = 91000 per year.
  250 words = 10-20 minutes of typing.
  Can you spare 20 minutes a day from your hectic life?

Then you can type a novel every year.

Notice I said 'type'. There's a lot more to writing a novel than bashing away at the keyboard, but that extra work is plotting, thinking and planning. These are things you can do at odd times of the day, and are mostly in the mind. Breaks at work, gaps between tutorials or lectures, recess or lunch times at school.

I once typed a scene on my cell phone whilst walking along a remote beach with my family. It's always possible to find that time somewhere, somehow.

— 7 —

Conclusion

7.1 It does get easier!

I've mentioned this before, but my first novel took years and years to finish. I started writing it in the middle of 1994, and after a couple of months I had 25,000 words. At the time I had no idea how long a novel was, and I used the newfangled internet thing to look it up. When the web search came back with the results about five minutes later (blame 9600 baud dialup) I was more than a little surprised. The average novel was 80,000 to 100,000 words. I'd just written 'The End' after barely finishing a quarter of a proper novel!

Our eldest daughter was born in December that year, and she was a bright, demanding little thing. She refused to sleep until 2am, and was usually up at 8. She needed constant stimulation, constant attention, and she spent all her waking hours frustrated at being trapped in a helpless little baby's body. She was sitting up in no time, and walking unaided at the age of eight months. She had a vocabulary of 250 words before her first birthday.

Why am I sharing this? Well, the day after our new

family got home from the hospital, I realised I wouldn't be writing anything for months, if not years. In fact, I didn't pick up that first novel until the end of 1998, almost five years later, and I laboured away like crazy and finished it by the end of '99.

So when I say my first novel took around five years to write, you can see why. (Our second daughter was born in 1997. Equally bright, she was much more laid back than her older sister. But . . . apart from working full time, I also started on my second university degree that year.)

I mention all of this because it really doesn't matter how long it takes to write your novel. Family is important, work is important, and sometimes you just have to fit your desire to write a novel around everything else.

And here's the good news. Your first novel *will* be a struggle. Your second will be a struggle too, but at least you'll know what it takes to finish one. By the time you hit your fourth or fifth novel you'll have come up with a good working method which cuts the time down considerably. Me, I'm currently writing my 17th, 18th and 19th novels, and while it's never going to be easy, the process has certainly become smoother and more refined.

So, what are the most important things I want you to get from this book?

•Don't worry about failing.

- When writing your first draft, don't fret about the quality of your work.
- The most important thing you can do is to *finish the first draft.*

7.2   Thank you!

If you got this far, I'd just like to say thanks for entrusting me with your precious time. I hope you got something, anything, out of my book, and I'm always happy to answer any questions you might have.

Simon Haynes

Perth, Western Australia
www.spacejock.com.au

— 8 —

Appendix I

8.1 Terminology

You'll see me refer to **scenes** from time to time. When I do, I'm referring to a portion of a chapter, usually separated from subsequent scenes with a marker or an extra blank line. (In ebooks I prefer to use a proper scene separator, such as * * *, because blank lines can be hard to spot.)

A **scene break** within a chapter indicates passing time, a jump to a new location, or a viewpoint switch to another character. A chapter always contains at least one scene, and sometimes two or more.

The **protagonist** is your primary character. That is, the person your book is about. In some novels there are multiple protagonists, all sharing equal billing.

The **antagonist** is the force confronting our protagonist. It could be a person, a faceless corporation, the police (if our antagonist has broken the law, or has been accused of a crime), a huge storm

... anything. In a romance novel the antagonist could simply be a rival. In a thriller it could be a mutated virus - or the people who created and released it.

Viewpoint, or point of view, indicates the person whose thoughts and observations we're sharing in the current scene.

• You can write your novel in first person, where the reader is *in* the story, and experiences everything as if they *were* the viewpoint character.

• Next, there's third person, where the reader can hear the viewpoint character's thoughts, and see what they see, but has no access to other characters.

• Finally, there's third party omniscient, where the reader can 'head hop' and listen to everyone's thoughts all the time.

8.2   A note about conflict

By conflict, I don't mean warfare! I'm talking about challenges. They can be trivial, like a missed appointment, or something huge like a threat to the whole galaxy. Conflict and challenges keep people reading, because they're eager to find out how things are resolved.

It's also worth considering the tools your protagonist has in his or her arsenal to face this challenge. You wouldn't send a soldier into a war zone with a plastic knife, and at the other extreme it would be silly to send a battle tank to settle a playground dispute between two kids at a primary school.

If your hero can overcome all challenges without lifting a finger, there's no conflict.

On the other hand, you want the stakes to be high, but not ludicrous.

By way of example, which sounds like a more interesting book:

The protagonist belongs to a secret government organisation which can push a button to defeat anyone, anywhere.

Or . . .

The protagonist belongs to a secret government organisation which has next to nothing in the way of resources, and has to get by on ingenuity and bravery.

Story is conflict, and conflict makes for good reading.

— 9 —

Appendix II

9.1 Writing sequels and series

If this is your very first novel, can I suggest that you don't set your heart on writing a series? Not yet, at least.

I made this mistake starting out. After writing one novel I couldn't find a publisher for, I set about writing a sequel. Eighteen months later, having finished the sequel, I wrote a third novel in the same series. Soon after, I realised I couldn't sell either of these to a publisher unless I sold the first novel.

Now, that novel was not only the first in this particular series, it was also the first novel I'd ever written. The plotting, the characters, the setting . . . to be charitable, they all needed work. The second and third books in the series were much better, but who was going to buy them? None of the people who tossed aside book one, that was for sure.

What I should have done was to bury the first book and start the series with book two.

Things have changed a lot these days, because instead of trying to attract an agent or a publisher, many authors are going straight to ebook. The issue remains, though: if your first book ends up being fairly average, and garners less than stellar reviews, writing more in the same series is a waste of time.

What I recommend you (and everyone else) should do is write standalone novels until the reviews and sales of a particular novel justify another book in the same series. Here's the thing: you will get better with every novel you write. Your fifth book will probably be twice as good as your first, and wouldn't it help your career so much more if readers of that fifth novel were clamouring for another one?

By all means, write the first in a series, but make sure it's self-contained. Publish it. Gauge the reaction. But perhaps start on the first book in a different series while the first is finding its feet.

Of course, if your first novel proves popular, by all means go ahead and work on the second. But be prepared to abandon it as a stand-alone. If it comes to that, you'll be very glad you didn't end it on a cliffhanger.

As I said, I made a similar mistake starting out. I put years of my life into the same series, writing more and more follow-on novels even though nobody was interested. My story might have been very different had I only written four different novels!

$$-\ 10\ -$$

Appendix III

10.1   Writing a novel with yWriter

I've mentioned yWriter a couple of times so far. I thought I'd spend a little time explaining how I write a novel using my own software, from the outlining stage to the very end.

I create 36 blank chapters in a new project, right-click chapter 9 and mark it as the start of the middle section. This turns the subsequent chapter headings orange. Then I right-click chapter 25 and mark that one as the start of the end section. That turns the rest of the chapter headings red. This gives me a visual guide right there in the chapter list.

Next I create a chapter called 'unused', right-click and mark it as 'Unused'. This will give me somewhere to move scenes I no longer want, and setting it to unused will prevent them being exported with the rest of my novel.

Finally, I add another new chapter and call it 'Notes', marking it as Unused as well. I can add a scene to this chapter and store information here... or I can use the 'Notes' tab on the main screen and enter my project notes there one by one.

By default, all new scenes are marked as 'Outline'. As I write each scene, I change the scene setting to Draft.

I also add my major characters to the project, with a very brief description.

There's a feature in yWriter where you can set deadline dates for each stage of your novel, from Draft through 1st and 2nd Edits, to Done. Once you set these dates, you can run off reports showing how much work you have to do, and how long you've got to do it. These are great for staying on track!

Eventually the goal is to have every scene marked as 'Done'. Now you can export the novel and send it to your beta readers.

yWriter is useful for proofing as well. It has a feature where you can export your novel to an RTF file, which you can send you a proof reader, and when you get it back you can import it again, preserving all the extra data like scene descriptions and so on. There are two important things to note here. First, the exported document contains special codes which identify the chapter and scene they belong to. If your proofreader goes through and deletes any of these, the document won't import properly. Second, you can't work on the novel until you import the version you exported. Well, you can, but you'll lose any changes you made.

To get around this, yWriter will export one or more chapters, and just re-import those. That means you can send someone the first ten chapters while you continue to work on chapters eleven and later.

yWriter has many other useful features, and the best place to learn more is on the official wiki page: sites.google.com/site/ywritersj

If you enjoyed this book, please leave a brief review at your online bookseller of choice. Thanks!

About the Author

Simon Haynes was born in England and grew up in Spain. His family moved to Australia when he was 16.

In addition to novels, Simon writes computer software. In fact, he writes computer software to help him write novels faster, which leaves him more time to improve his writing software. And write novels faster. (www.spacejock.com/yWriter.html)

Simon's goal is to write fifteen novels before someone takes his keyboard away.

Update 2018: goal achieved and I still have my keyboard!
New goal: write thirty novels.

Simon's website is spacejock.com.au

For info on new releases and updates:

spacejock.com.au/MLNF.html

Acknowledgements

To everyone who's helped me with my novels over the years thanks for the awesome help and support!

THE HAL SPACEJOCK SERIES

"Fast, funny, quirky, enthralling comedy adventure"
Tom Vest

A ROBOT NAMED CLUNK

A science fiction comedy

SIMON HAYNES

"Brilliantly quirky, wildly absurd"

"The perfect blend of adventure, conflict and laughable moments"

In a vast, inhabited galaxy, two corrupt businessmen are battling each other for supremacy. At stake is a lucrative contract, and these ruthless antagonists will not quit until one of them takes the prize.

Clunk, an elderly robot, and Hal Spacejock, a penniless cargo pilot, are the latest worthless pawns to be sucked in by these corrupt businessmen. Sucked in, chewed up and spat out again.

But this time the pawns are fighting back. This time, the little guys have had enough.

Buckle up for mayhem, mischief and payback as the creaky old robot and the down-on-his-luck space pilot turn the tables on the bad guys.

With lashings of accidental destruction, random mechanical breakdowns and some really lousy flying, Hal and Clunk are bound to come out on top.

Eventually... sort of.

"Brilliantly quirky, wildly absurd"

  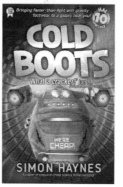

Ebook and Trade Paperback

THE
HARRIET WALSH
SERIES

It's Harriet Walsh's first day as a Peace Force trainee, and she's given a simulated case to solve. Simulated, because Dismolle is a peaceful planet and there's absolutely no crime.

Well, almost no crime.

You see, Harriet's found a genuine case to investigate, and she's hot on the trail of a real live suspect.

Which is a shame, because her crime-fighting computer is so basic it doesn't even have solitaire.

Coming 2020

Ebook and Trade Paperback

THe
HAL JUNIOR
SERIES

Hal Junior lives aboard a futuristic space station. His mum is chief scientist, his dad cleans air filters and his best mate is Stephen 'Stinky' Binn.

As for Hal ... he's a bit of a trouble magnet. He means well, but his wild schemes and crazy plans never turn out as expected!

Hal Junior: The Secret Signal features mayhem and laughs, daring and intrigue ... plus a home-made space cannon!

THE
DRAGON & CHIPS
TRILOGY

Ebook and Trade Paperback

A mild-mannered old robot has just been transported to a medieval kingdom, and things are quickly going from bad to worse:

A homicidal knight is after his blood - or the robot equivalent.

A greedy queen wants to bend him to her will.

A conniving Master of Spies is hatching his own devious plan for the mechanical marvel.

And worst of all, there's nowhere to get a recharge!

"Laugh after laugh, dark in places but the humour punches through. Amazing!"

Printed in Great Britain
by Amazon